Damien as a young priest.

FATHER DAMIEN is Molokai. He is Molokai as the rock-bound hills and verdant palms are Molokai. He is Molokai as festering, leprous sores are Molokai. He is Molokai as the turbulent breakers that foam endlessly on its beaches. Father Damien is Molokai.

Joseph de Veuster was the son of an ambitious man. A merchant, a man of commerce, a trader in commodities: this was the career the ambitious father shaped for the son born to him on January 3, 1840, at Tremeloo in Belgium.

But bartering for profit in gold was to Joseph a vain pursuit when souls that might be golden with Grace were rusting in a pool of sin. Souls, he knew, were his vocation. In the novitiate of the Fathers of the Sacred Hearts of Jesus and Mary in Louvain, he studied for souls.

He was only in Minor Orders when sent to the Hawaiian Islands and was ordained priest in Honolulu on March 19, 1864, taking the name of Father Damien. For nine years, Father Damien sailed the Pacific seas in and about these Islands and learned of Molokai with its six hundred lepers who lay rotting help-

(Continued on back flap)

lessly on its shores. At his own request they became the vineyard of his labors.

Molokai's weather-knarled shacks suddenly gave place to clean white huts, sordid refuse and contagious squalor yielded to the ways of sanitation; the catafalque of despair was flung aside to reveal the white garment of hope. All this as the strong hands and heart and mind of Father Damien plied unswervingly to his own White Martyrdom.

When the labors of twelve years had closed, a new and shorter chapter opened to Father Damien, for he, too, was touched by the Hand of God and became, like his children, a leper. Three years later, April 15, 1888, his disintegrating, pain-ridden body unshackled its soul to his Savior.

Father Damien has become for mankind a symbol . . . an undying sign of unreckoning courage, life-consuming zeal and Christ-like compassion. He was truly, in the words of Crashaw, one of those

Ripe men of martyrdom, that could reach down
With strong arms their triumphant crown;
Such as could with lusty breath,
Speak loud into the face of Death.

Damien shortly before he died.

FATHER DAMIEN de VEUSTER

WHITE
MARTYRDOM

by

JOHN HENAGHAN

WHITE MARTYRDOM

By

The Rev. John Henaghan

of the

Society of St. Columban

St. Columban's, Milton, Mass.

Silver Creek, N. Y.   Bristol, R. I.

San Diego, Cal.   Los Angeles, Cal.

St. Columbans, Nebraska

Nihil Obstat

HUGH F. BLUNT, LL.D.

Diocesan Censor

Imprimatur

✠ RICHARD J. CUSHING, D.D., LL.D.

Archbishop of Boston

June 10, 1946

To see the infinite pity of this place,
The mangled limb, the devastated face,
The innocent sufferer smiling at the rod—
The fool were tempted to deny his God.

He sees, he shrinks. But if he gaze again,
Lo, beauty springing from the breast of pain!
He marks the Sisters on the mournful shores;
And even a fool is silent and adores.

—*Robert Louis Stevenson*

CONTENTS

FOREWORD

by the
Most Reverend Richard J. Cushing, D.D.
Archbishop of Boston

FATHER DAMIEN'S life has often been told, but this is the first time the telling has been done by a man who approaches Damien's own stature. When Father John Henaghan, St. Columban missionary and author of WHITE MARTYRDOM, selected as his subject the Apostle of the Lepers, there was a divine fitness in his choice. It is not often a confessor of the Faith has for his biographer a priest who would later be put to death preaching the Faith. Father Damien died the slow martyrdom of leprosy. Father Henaghan and his St. Columban companions* perished like the early Christians in prison by fire and by sword.

The life and death of Father Damien, the hero of this story, and the life and death of Father Henaghan, the writer of the story, give us, between them, the completeness of the Cross. Even in the annals of the missions, such coincidence and combination are rare.

*Editor's Note: Fathers John Henaghan, Patrick Kelly, Peter Fallon, Joseph Monaghan and Francis V. Douglas, were put to death prior to the liberation of the Philippine Islands in February, 1945. Their companion, Father John Lalor, was killed by a shell while attending the wounded.

1

"There is red martyrdom and white martyrdom," writes Father Henaghan in his book, quoting from the parchment of an old Irish monk. That old Irish monk, centuries ago, was unconsciously uttering a prophecy to be fulfilled by many of his race. Father Henaghan is one more to a list already long. And when he picked those words of that wise old monk's book, did he feel that before many months he would add to the white martyrdom of saintly Damien the red blood of his own noble heart?

WHITE MARTYRDOM is a treasury of these two beautiful lives. This alone gives it high claim as a classic of the missions and ensures for it a permanent place in the chronicles of men who have done greatly and died for God.

We welcome its publication by Father Henaghan's own Community of the St. Columban Fathers, Milton, Mass., within the Archdiocese of Boston. We predict for it an immediate and continued popularity. It is our prayer that the moving message of WHITE MARTYRDOM may prove an inspiration to many young men of the Archdiocese of Boston and elsewhere to follow such leaders to the White Harvest now awaiting them in foreign fields.

+ Richard J Cushing

BIOGRAPHICAL SKETCH

THE MAN who wrote this life of Damien of Molokai, and who for fifteen years was a monthly contributor to St. Columban's mission magazine *The Far East,* is dead. He was among those killed in Manila in February, 1945. But his words, written and spoken, will live in many a soul for many a day. So will his personal influence among those who knew him. Some of these feel that never in a lifetime have they known anyone whose heart was more closely attuned to the Heart of Christ than was Father John Henaghan's.

His great natural gifts took fire from his burning love of Christ. How that dark head would lift, and the sensitive face would light up, and the deep voice would change from quiet slowness to ringing, rousing eloquence, when he spoke of the sufferings of Our Lord or the Mass or Nazareth or the Blessed Mother! How he kindled enthusiasm for the missions, for the Cause of Christ everywhere!

He wrote and spoke as he lived, without a trace of self-consciousness, with utter sincerity. The fire in his heart was real and it never grew cold. He was incapable of rigidity or exaggeration in any form. His humor was as genuine, as distinctive and as delightful as his spirituality.

To Father Henaghan, as a young curate in the West of Ireland, as a professor among St. Columban's first students in Dalgan Park, in a Manila parish, life was simply active, intimate friendship with the living Christ. His sympathy for sufferers and sinners, his constant thought of the poor, his unresting zeal for souls, his quick understanding of every human need, were all inspired by his personal attachment to his Divine Friend.

In a letter of 1940, never intended for publication, one of Father Henaghan's fellow-priests wrote about him as follows: "He has left his impression on Manila in a way that few people know. What a wonderfully full character he is! I never knew him properly until I went to the Philippines. It was worth while going there just for that. It will be a memory to treasure for the rest of my life."

Many a grieving voice will echo those words today.

Father Henaghan has died a death that he would have humbly honored in another man. He died, even as Damien died, a martyr to a cause he loved and cherished—the cause of the missions.

May he enter swiftly into the joy of his Lord, Who has not called him servant but friend.

Patrick O'Connor

St. Columban's Seminary
Milton, Mass.

DEDICATION

"LIKE the spray on the shore 'neath the cliff,
Like the dew on the hill or the breath of the wind
From the white sails that pant o'er the sea,
Or the whisper of tales that are told though
*   their tellers be still,*
Is their fame in my ear, is their glory to me."

THERE is always a strange fascination in pondering
the story of heroic unselfish lives—something which,
while lifting us up to a higher plane, and coming
with an appeal to the heroic in ourselves, bids us
wish that even though only in some far-off way, it
may be our privilege to claim kinship and brotherhood with them. Courage, in no matter what form
shown, always appeals to men.

Each country has its heroes whose names are house-
hold words—souls who proved they loved truth above
falsehood, justice above injustice, and their country's
cause above life itself. For each of these there is a
unique chord on which to sound the song of praise.
Each subject, too, has its own note of pathos. But what
note shall one strike in approaching the life of Father
Damien, the apostle of the lepers, the martyr of far-
away Molokai? Will it be a note of tender pathos we
shall strike as we recount the incidents that stand out
in the life-story of one whose daily portion it was to

witness and to share in the living death of these pitiable sufferers—the lepers? No, though if one wrote of the horrors of the lepers' life alone it would be a picture too sad to be portrayed in human words.

Will it be a note of triumph and gladness? Yes, it shall be so. For we write not in the tones of pagan despair, but with the glad hopefulness of Christianity, as we tell the story of a man who in the springtime of his life and in the glory of his days went down to a living death—of a man who lit up all the vileness and abominations of Molokai with the torch of Christian hope—of a man who, bravely and unafraid, faced all the horrors of leprosy, toiling and sweating in disease-infested huts, and in the end dying a victim to his zeal.

We quote from a letter whose paper has turned brown and of which the ink has almost faded—"My vocation was more of a surprise to myself than to anyone else and I cannot say it was a pleasant surprise either, but I felt convinced that God wanted me and I did not dare refuse His call. I decided that I would rather go to Molokai to work for the lepers there than any place else . . . my real reason for becoming a Franciscan was of course that these Sisters were the ones who went to Hawaii in 1883 to help Father Damien who was then a leper himself. I entered the Convent on the Feast of the Sacred Heart, 1913, and from that day up to the present I have been homesick for the fair hills of Holy Ireland—not that I am not happy, and never happier than when I am with our dear lepers, but, personally, no one but God Himself or His work could induce me to live outside Ireland. In April, 1915, I realized my ambition to go to Molokai amongst the lepers in the place sanctified by Father Damien's long martyrdom.

"After eighteen privileged months in Molokai I was transferred to the Settlement for the children of the lepers on Molokai. I had the pleasure of many a talk with our saintly Mother Marianne who brought the first band of Sisters here to take care of the lepers; Mother was old, of course, when I was with her, but her memory was good and her experience of life in Hawaii in the latter part of the 19th century was wonderfully interesting. It was she who put Father Damien into his coffin when he died in 1889 . . .

"Robert Stevenson was also an intimate friend of the Sisters and even yet a few of the old patients remember him and speak of him with great affection. He made himself a real friend to those poor leper girls and loved to play games with them, and then, when he was quite exhausted with his exertions, he used to lie down on the grass by Mother's chair—to get scolded for over-exerting himself and running the risk of a hemorrhage . . ."

How many souls have been stirred by the heroism of this man who willingly became a leper for the sake of lepers because the love of God burned strongly within his soul—this Sister whose words we have quoted above—, R. L. Stevenson, and countless others inside and outside the Catholic Church! Many a one since, at the thought of that unpretentious priest in a worn cassock, giving all—his body and his life—for God's most abandoned poor, has obtained strength to face the lonely hours of suffering and has come to a clearer understanding of Christ, our Lord.

Father Damien's absolute giving of himself has shown clearly what Christ's own love was like, and has roused souls from their easy, comfortable way of thought and living to see the Lord in the least of His brethren. Damien has brought disturbance into thoughtless lives and has aroused a great unrest within the soul which can be quieted into peace only by an absolute surrender to Christ and His poor suffering ones.

There is no healing for the world save in that faith and love that sees in the suffering members of our common humanity "the temples of the Holy Ghost," and our real brethren in the Lord. Damien preached the true Brotherhood of Man, in the red wounds of the God-Man on the Cross.

WHITE MARTYRDOM

SOIL OF HEROES

*J*OSEPH DE VEUSTER was born January 3, 1840, in the little village of Tremoloo, six miles from the University town of Louvain, Belgium. It is a rich, flat country, without break or rising ground on the horizon, yet with no monotony, due to the patch-work of fields, continually changing in size and color, and verdant with the varied crops pressed from its fertile soil by the unremitting toil of the hardy Belgian farmers. His parents were of the peasant class—simple, pious, hard-working folks—not a bad stock for producing heroes. "Blue blood is putrid blood, the people's blood is red."

There is not much recorded about him as a boy. Each family lived a happy peaceful life, observing the law of God and treating with those around in friendly spirit as becomes children of a common Father, bound by ties of a common Faith. There is nothing much to record of a childhood spent in an atmosphere of peace and beauty, close to a loving mother and a stern but kindly father. A silent sort of lad was Joseph, fond of roaming through the fields, very useful and handy about the house, drinking in his religion from his mother while in the evenings he sat with his brothers and sisters around the open fire blazing in the large, cheerful kitchen. Silently and delightedly he listened while she told them stories of the great heroes of God, whose memories live in shrine and crypt, of the martyrs who braved the agonies of the rack, and the slow roasting on the gridiron to profess the Faith, to defend God's glory, or rescue an enslaved fellow-Christian from the clutches of the infidel. Some one has written that the grandest school in Ireland is at an Irish mother's knee. It is true of every land. Mothers, wherever they are, are the custodians of a nation's greatness.

The whole setting of Damien's life is suggested to us in Millet's picture of the "Angelus" where we see the two peasants standing with bowed heads against the Autumn glow, and we can almost hear the Angelus' bell ringing out over the furrowed field its message of joy to simple hearts.

At one time, it was 'Fair Day' in the village. Joseph disappeared . . . was lost. His parents sought him. At the end of the day he was finally discovered in the village chapel, nestling close to the altar. "The thoughts of youth are long, long thoughts." What were the thoughts that filled Damien's soul as he prayed in the half-light of that summer evening long ago, having left the noise, the bustle, the fun and jollity of the Fair grounds for the soul-satisfying silence of the dim-lighted church? Had he any dreamings of great things to do, any presentiments?

He was passionately fond of skating. His old school-fellows in Tremoloo loved to recount tales of his prowess on the skates, an ability which won him the coveted title of local champion on the rink. He would fly on wings of steel for miles on miles along the frozen canals, past the windmills and the villages, full of the joy of rapturous life, exulting in his youth, gulping down great draughts of love for his own places, for home, and for the beautiful Belgian skies above him.

We can easily picture to ourselves what a big-hearted fellow he was, ready to turn his hand to anything—rumor had it that he often assisted the sexton in the village church in the gloomy task of digging the graves in the cemetery hard by, thus unwittingly gaining experience that was to serve him well in the future! His youth was like that of most normal boys, the only trait which seemed to mark him off from his fellows was a love for solitude accentuated by the constant awareness of God which stood him in good stead in his later life. He was gentle as a lamb, with a gentleness only possessed by the strong. Already there burned within him the clear white flame of a unique and powerful personality.

Having absorbed in his native village all the book-learning the local school-master could impart, Joseph was sent to an Academy of higher learning in the town of Braine-le-Comte in the province of Hainault. Here he grew familiar with the French language, for as yet he had spoken only Flemish, a provincial language. Joseph was lonely in this town school, and the few hours free from studies he devoted to long walks into the country. Silence, prayer and solitude were gradually preparing De Veuster to listen to the call sounding within his soul, the vocation to the service of God and neighbor.

There is no hard and fast rule as to what makes for happiness, for perfection. What suits one soul would not suit another. God leads us by strange ways to what is best for us, eternally. Damien understood this and prepared the soil of his heart for the divine seed. In the Christian atmosphere which surrounded him he sensed the high purpose of his creation, and already he was prepared to be ever as 'a docile instrument in the hands of a skillful workman.'

After a 'mission' given by the Redemptorist Fathers in the parish church of Braine-le-Comte, Joseph came home one evening and instead of retiring to rest he remained the whole night at his bedside praying. "And it came to pass in those days that He went out into a mountain . . . and He passed the whole night in the prayer of God, and when day was come He called unto Him whom He would Himself. And they came to him." Thus simply is the story of Divine Vocation portrayed in the holy Gospel narrative. Thus simply and none the less profoundly is it reproduced in every heart attuned to the gentle whisper of the spirit of God. A vocation always remains a mystery . . . always the secret of the King. God calls people in different ways. To some He whispers; others he rouses with a trumpet; there are doors that will not yield except to very hard blows. Sometimes He does not speak at all, and only in the silence of our soul do we realize that His summons is there.

Damien heard and with the straightforward candor of the pure of heart, he welcomed the call, only stopping to enquire: "Lord, what wilt Thou have me to do?"

MISSIONARY VOCATION

*A*T FIRST Joseph de Veuster had thoughts of entering among the Trappists, a most severe and austere branch of the Cistercians, whose members vow to observe perpetual silence, hard manual labor, and continual prayer. Before taking any decisive step, however, he wrote to his brother Pamphile, who was at this time pursuing his theological studies among the Picpus Fathers, as the Congregation of the Sacred Hearts of Jesus and Mary was familiarly known.

With brotherly understanding the young cleric pointed out to his ardent correspondent the sublime functions of the 'mixed' life wherein the example of the Divine Saviour is more particularly followed: the Hidden life of prayer, the Public life of service, the Sacrificial life of daily mortification. With his usual directness of purpose Joseph hearkened to the advice and offered himself to the Missionary Society where his elder brother had preceded him. Bidding farewell to home and loved ones he went at once to the Novitiate and set himself to the task of preparing for the service of God.

On his entering, following the custom of the Order, he was permitted to choose a new name. Damien was the one he chose. Early in the fourth century, Damien, a famous physician of Cilicia, served well the suffering members of Christ, and in the end laid down his life a martyr in the cause of God. What renown will Joseph De Veuster bring to this name?

During the period devoted to Novitiate training he learned his stern lesson well . . . not in a day does any man grow great, or evil, for that matter, but it is the sure result of the silent years, the slow imperceptible development of the man. Damien grew. He made astounding discoveries of the vast spiritual world within himself. And in no manner did he lose the exultant spirit of his boyhood dreams. He was then nineteen years old, of splendid physique, with a fine, frank, handsome face crowned with dark curly hair, his countenance glowing with high hopes and the ardours of his young ambition. He kept ever true to the vision, and allowed the years to do their work of ripening him for the fulfillment of the dream. He had no notion as yet of what that dream might be.

In one of his easy, familiar letters to his parents, he mentions a visit paid the Community by one of their missionary bishops from a far-flung outpost of Christianity in Oceania:

"I believe this zealous missionary will shortly return thence, and may possibly take some of us with him. Would you not be happy if I were one? . . . "

It so happened, indeed, that at this time his brother Pamphile, now a priest, fell ill just as the band of missionaries of which he was a member were starting for their mission in the South Seas. Damien, though as yet only a student, volunteered to take his place. He was accepted. "For the Sandwich Islands—Damien De Veuster." Without much preparation, and with his natural directness he bade farewell to home and loved ones and landed in the Sandwich Islands in 1863. He was ordained in Honolulu in 1864. He was then only twenty-three years of age.

"Who lives for Christ must tread His way,
Leave self and all the world behind,
Press ever up and on, and serve
His kind with single mind.

No easy way—rough-strewn with thorns,
And wearisome the path He trod,
But His way is the only way
That leads men back to God.

And lonesome oft, and often dark
With shame and outcastry and scorn,
And at the end perhaps a cross
And many a crown of thorn."

SCENE OF CONFLICT

*T*HESE ISLANDS, 'mystic Isles
of the South Seas,' to which Damien came, lie about
half-way between America and the Philippines, in
the Pacific Ocean. They were discovered in 1778 by
Captain Cook, though a prior claim is made by some
in favor of the Spaniards who supposedly settled on
the island of Hawaii as early as 1555. These islands
are famous for their delightful climate, the fertility
of their soil, the abundance of their tropical flora.
They have been well called the 'Paradise of the Pacific,' a place to enter with a song upon one's lips,
seeing veritable isles of happiness and joy.

Romance hangs round the very name of the South
Sea Islands, and it requires some lord of language to
do justice to these gardens of delight. They appear to
the traveler from sterner climes like some Fairy
Isles of dreamland, or Tir'na'nog, or those fabled
isles which the Arran fisherman sees from his *curragh*
as the sun goes down.

"One's first glimpse of the South Seas," writes R.
L. Stevenson, "is a memory apart and touches a

virginity of sense. There are mountains and rivers and delicious streams tumbling down precipices to the deep blue sea; dark green groves run down to the water's edge; here and there volcanic rocks reach right down to the sea and are hollowed out into fantastic caverns by the surf. Tropical ferns grow to a height of fourteen feet; and the gardens are rich with flowers and foliage. A scene of fine, wild, volcanic beauty—coconut palms, with tall hibiscus, oleander in profusion and in every variety of color, abundance of delicious fruits, pineapples so tender that you can eat them with a spoon, papaya, watermelon, bananas, alligator pears, all there for the taking. Balmy airs are always blowing, the summer seas flashing in the sun. Green of every hue lends variety to the landscape while thousands of huge blossoms scatter their overpowering fragrance on the sunlit air. It is a land grown wanton with loveliness—a lotus isle where men forget their cares and like the travelers in Ulysses' story, having once tasted of its beauty, forget their home and kindred, content to live there in indolent luxury."

The Hawaiians are a fine muscular race, of velvety-brown skin and good features, very hospitable, easily moved to happiness or tears, with a kindliness, a generosity, a readiness to forgive and forget without parallel.

The opening up of the Islands brought many Europeans, not always with profit, so that now the native Hawaiian seems lost in the crowd of foreigners, both Oriental and European. They came from every clime—men who found America too 'hot' for them, men in search of a fortune or pleasure, skulkers from life's battles, men 'on the rocks'—all these found the air of the Islands suitable to their tastes.

Stevenson, in a telling paragraph, describes the foreign element in Hawaii. "Throughout the island world of the Pacific, are scattered men of many European races and from almost every grade of society, carrying on ceaseless activity and disseminating disease. Some prosper, some vegetate, some have mounted the steps of thrones and owned islands and navies, others again must marry for a livelihood; and dressed like natives but still retaining some foreign element of gait or attitude, still perhaps with some relic (such as one eye-glass) of the officer or the gentleman, they sprawl in palm-leaf verandas and entertain an island audience with memories of the music-hall. There are others again, less pliable, less capable, less fortunate, less base perhaps, who continue in these isles of plenty to lack bread." So much for the human element of the Islands.

SHADOWS

$\mathcal{F}$ATHER DAMIEN'S mission was in Hawaii—the largest of the Sandwich group. The Islands until recently were pagan, full of dark rites, of cruelties, and pitiful strivings after the unknown God. However, in this particular 'near-Paradise' where Damien's first years were to be spent, the people had taken kindly to Catholicism and several resident priests had already built a cathedral as well as a number of small chapels. Deposited finally in his parish in the district of Puno he takes time out to write a description of the surroundings to his priest-brother Pamphile. "Hawaii, the island on which I am stationed, is as large as Belgium, if not larger.

"In the center are three volcanoes, two of which appear to be extinct. The third is still active and it is in the neighborhood of this that Providence has destined me to be placed. From one end of my district to the other, one has to walk on lava . . . I think I shall require from three to four days to get from one end to the other. In every direction there are little villages scattered about, and for seven or eight years there has been no resident priest. The Bishop told me the mission was quite in its infancy. Indeed, I found no church in which to say Mass, but two are now in the course of construction."

Damien's life as a young missionary was hard. There were many demands upon his time. His hand was every ready for a grown man's work. His letters home at this period were frequent, telling of his life, of his activities, of the souls to be comforted, of the churches to be built, and always asking for a remembrance in prayers. He was delighted with the people, so gentle, so pleasant-mannered, so hospitable. He was the same affectionate Joseph as of old, recalling in his letters all the little details of his childhood memories, showing that the leagues of sea could not blot out the picture he knew so well.

He mentions in one of these letters the appalling spread of leprosy among the poor people he met in the course of his ministry, and ended by asking prayers—like the humble man he was—ever conscious of his soul's deep needs. "In general, I have much bother, and little consolation, and it is only by God's grace I can find my yoke sweet and my burden light." And again he writes: "Let us be in the hands of God as tools in the hands of a skillful workman . . . When I get a little unwell I congratulate myself that the end is near, but I am content with my lot, only let perseverance crown my work. Pray for me. Damien." Note the little human querulousness, the complaint. But the end is not yet. He has harder roads to travel. He is unconscious of what the future holds, but a capacity for sacrifice calls for the opportunity for sacrifice—and for this Damien has placed himself, always ready 'as a tool in the hands of a skillful workman.'

Nothing was capable of cooling the ardor of his missionary zeal which was enkindled at the Holy Sacrifice of the Mass, and in his intimate communings with the Blessed Sacrament. "Jesus Christ is in an especial manner with missionaries," he wrote, "so I place all my confidence in Him Who has accepted my offering and who daily nourishes me with His Body and Blood." Soon his zeal and endurance was to be tested; the white flame of his pure priestly sacrifice would burn in a still nobler service and in a more utter resemblance to his Lord.

Suddenly, in the midst of this earthly paradise, a shadow loomed spectre-like. With the rapidity of a thunder-clap, the gathering storm broke over the once-so-happy island. There is no reliable account of how the dreadful blight was first brought in, but it is certain that living conditions in Hawaii caused its rapid spread.

Leprosy came like a blow on these Hawaiian people and they fell before its rancid breath. There seemed no escape. Men fled; homes were broken up, the Government grew alarmed and ordered all those afflicted with the disease to be detained in the island of Molokai. When this edict went forth, a wail of sorrow and of grief was heard throughout the

Archipelago. All the physical loveliness of the place was lost and swept from the mind by the remembrance of the gruesome fact that among these many people leprosy stalked as a spectre at a feast. There were cries of anguish and despair—lepers were hunted like convicts and carried off, no matter how high their station in life, no matter who the person—grown man, or tender maiden, or helpless child.

Damien saw some of his parishioners being hurried off—saw the terrible distress and misery of the poor people—and these scenes so heartrending were indelibly impressed on his mind and treasured there. His thoughts turned often to the unfortunate outcasts in the distant island of Molokai, and every day at the altar of the Mass he prayed God to comfort them. He tells us of the strong presentiment he felt at this time that he should soon rejoin his parishioners in that lonely island prison. He speaks of 'our mutual attachment' and listen: "a word, a mere word uttered laughingly on the subject was sufficient to cause an emotion in him. Just a trembling of the heart-strings . . . a sense of longing . . . stirred by that word 'Molokai'."

HOUR OF SACRIFICE

*H*E WAS coming near the hour of his sacrifice. It happened simply, like this: The Bishop was consecrating a chapel in Maui, and Damien with several of his brother priests was invited to be present at the ceremony. He tells us that as he left his parish that morning an interior voice kept telling him he should never again see his beloved flock nor the four beautiful chapels he had built for their souls' needs. He admits there were tears in his eyes as he threw a last glance at his loved district of Kohala. "Tears, idle tears, I wonder what they mean?"

The consecration of the little church in Maui was a truly magnificent ceremony and at its close the zealous bishop took the opportunity at dinner for a close and intimate conference with his devoted priests. In the course of his talk he touched on the spiritual misery of the unfortunate lepers in Molokai. Damien's heart leaped within him. His chance had come. The hour of his sacrifice. "My Lord," he said quietly across the dinner table, "if you will be kind enough to allow it, I will go to Molokai and labor for the poor lepers." The offer was at once accepted and that day, without any farewells, without any preparation, just as he was, Damien went to his sacrifice. That evening a steamer sailed from the little island of Maui, with Damien and his Bishop aboard. On arriving at Honolulu, they found a crowd of lepers huddled on the shore, waiting to be shipped that same evening to the dismal colony. And here, without even time to collect a few personal belongings, having nothing but an extra shirt and his breviary, he embarked on the inter-island vessel, the *Kilanea*, amidst the sounds of wailing, and the mournful dirges which punctuated the last good-byes from the watchers on the shore.

Damien was young. Life was all before him. The rich blood of health ran in his veins. But he went without a word, no fanfare, no waving of flags, no excitement. All through the night Damien listened to the human weeping, mingled with the bellowing of the cattle also transported on that vessel of despair. Yet there must have been a fluttering among the angels of God as they looked down upon that poor man who went out to fight, single-handed and alone, against grim despair and the cold terrors of Molokai.

In the cold grey dawn the steamer launched him, friendless, unsheltered, without a single earthly possession, on the lonely promontory . . . and went on its way. What were his thoughts as he touched the accursed shore of his island prison? The sun rose in a golden glow, while Damien watched the ship depart. He was indeed alone. It was hard to face the revolting sight of those distorted forms who came onto the beach to tender him a greeting. But these were his parishioners now.

One of the most touching incidents in the life of St. Francis of Assisi is thus described by his biographer. Perhaps it could also be written of Damien:

"The day of days came to Francis out on the plain. He had been riding and was returning to the city when a leper stood in his way, supplicating an alms. At the sight of his loathsome disfigurement the very soul of Francis sickened as it did in the presence of all ugly disease . . . At an earlier time he would have flung out his alms and passed quickly on. But to-day a great wave of pity swept over him and would not let him pass. He reined in his horse and dismounted, and as he courteously placed his alms in the beggar's hand he took the hand and kissed it. Then clasping the leper in his arms, he himself received from the leper the kiss of peace. From that moment Francis never again looked back upon the old ways; in the leper's embrace he plighted his troth to a new life in which love of Christ and service of the poor alone commanded his liege service. In his gratitude Francis looked upon the lepers as his peculiar charge; he visited their settlements and brought them alms; and always as he gave his alms he kissed their hands."

Damien slept the first night, and many another

dreary night, under a tree, alone with that dread pestilence, and looking forward with what pitiful shrinking of dread, God alone knows, to a life-time of dressing sores and fast-decaying stumps. On the morrow he rose refreshed, for the night had mercifully effaced the visible horrors of the first day, and as he was not a man to waste time in regrets or memories, he applied himself to the tremendous task before him.

From now on the Crucifix would become a Living Thing to his spirit—and the center of all living things.

MOLOKAI, AHINA!

*M*OLOKAI, seen from a distance, on a passing ship, seems like a lotus-isle that knows not life's commotion—a blest "No-Man's Land," yet it is a name which when mentioned among the South Seas causes laughter to die on the lips and fear to clutch at the heart. Molokai Ahina—grey, lofty and most desolate land. It calls up all the horrors of a prison. It means the separation of husband from wife, of child from its mother, and the young man from his bride. It is an abode of gloom.

On near approach it shows to be a land beetling, gloomy and inhospitable. It is a wedge-shaped island, thirty miles long by seven in width, rising gradually from the sea with cliffs upon its northern side. Between these cliffs and the sea is situated the Leper Colony. It is thus cut off from the rest of the islands. Here on this little patch of ground was Damien's battleplace.

Stevenson, visiting it after Damien's death, wrote: "It was a pitiful place to live in . . . and a hell to die in." Damien himself tells us that as he stepped on the island that first day he said to himself: "Now, Joseph, my boy, here is your life-work." When he found time he wrote a lengthy letter to his brother: "God has chosen your unworthy brother to assist these poor people attacked by that terrible malady so often mentioned in the Gospel—leprosy. For the last ten years the plague has been spreading in the islands, and at last the Government found itself obliged to isolate those affected with it.

"Shut up between inaccessible cliffs and the sea, these unfortunate creatures are condemned to perpetual exile. A priest was wanted to succor them, but here was a difficulty; the priest who is placed here must consider himself shut up with the lepers for the rest of his life. So remembering that on the day of my Profession, I had already put myself under a funeral pall, I offered myself to His Lordship to meet, if he thought it well, this second death. Consequently, on May eleventh, a steamer landed me here . . . I found on my arrival no house to shelter me. I lived for a long time under the shelter of a tree, not wishing to sleep under the same roof as the lepers.

"Later on, the whites of Honolulu helped me with their substance, and so I was enabled to build a hut sixteen feet long and ten wide, where I am now writing these lines. Well, I have been here six months surrounded by lepers and so far I have not caught the infection. I consider this shows the special protection of our good God and the Blessed Virgin Mary."

CURSE OF THE AGES

$\mathcal{F}$ROM THE earliest times, this most repulsive disease was looked upon among both Jews and Gentiles as a special curse from God. It was known in Egypt, India and Japan long centuries before the coming of Christ. We learn from the Bible how it was spread among the Jews. No scientific remedies were attempted once a man was infected, but every means within the scope of human knowledge was requisitioned to prevent contagion. For the safeguarding of the general health then, segregation of the infected was the rigidly prescribed preventative.

The laws of the Jews were very strict in their treatment of the leper. He was banished from the campus and cities of men, hunted from the haunts of friends, pelted with stones from field to field, condemned to wander among the tombs and solitary places, coming in search of food—like some beast of prey—at nightfall. Men shrank from his presence, and children fled him.

It did not matter who he was or what his rank.

It was the same unpitying law for all, the same living death. Every leper was accursed. He was ordered to cry out "Unclean, unclean, make room for the leper." Rags and tears were his portion, death his only friend. The lepers had to wear a special garb, and give notice of their approach. They were forbidden to enter mills, churches, or attend fairs or markets. Their dwelling must be in the open country, far from men and the roads.

With the lapse of centuries, and particularly at the time of the Crusades, leprosy spread over Europe. It was found in the huts of the poor and in the palaces of Kings. Two English monarchs died of the disease. In the Middle Ages, all over Europe, there were leper houses attached to the monasteries, for though much has been written adversely concerning the Church in medieval times, yet it was the Church through her priesthood that successfully wiped out leprosy in Europe. "All who come shall be welcomed as though they were Christ" was the rule in these monastic lazars. By the end of the fifteenth century the disease was practically wiped out of Europe. It is now scarcely ever heard of except in the East and the islands of the Pacific.

There are three kinds of leprosy. One form causes the whole body to become a ghastly white, and the general health is affected. In another, the extremities become insensible to pain and gradually slough away with sores until the whole body is crippled. The third kind is distinguished by disfiguration and discoloration, the joints of the fingers drop off one by one like rotten twigs. Many of the poor sufferers become blind and crawl about as best they can. In some, the throat becomes attacked, the voice sounds hollow and dies away, and from all emanate the corpse-like smell of decaying flesh.

As a rule the lepers do not suffer any extraordinary pain except in advanced stages. Frequently the face becomes horribly disfigured with sores and swellings, and, strange to relate, these poor victims have a mania for looking at themselves in the mirror. Laudable and persistent efforts have been made since the days of Damien to effect a permanent cure for this most tragic and pitiful of diseases, but the poor, ignorant, superstitious natives who are always the chief victims sometimes defer treatment until it is too late.

SHEPHERD OF OUTCASTS

*A*ND NOW these outcasts of society were to become Damien's friends, his only familiars. We can picture him waiting for that first dawn which would reveal to him the full extent of the sacrifice before him. Let us listen to Stevenson as he describes the task: "You will say perhaps," he writes, "that I am too sensitive, that sights as painful abound in cancer hospitals, and are confronted daily by doctors and nurses. I have long learned to admire the doctors and nurses. But there is no cancer hospital as large and populous as Kalanao. And what daunts the onlookers is the monstrous sum of human suffering by which he stands surrounded . . .

"Lastly, no doctor is asked to enter once and for all the doors of the Gehenna. They do not say farewell. They do not abandon hope on its sad threshold. They go but for a time to their high calling, and look forward as they go, to ultimate relief, recreation and rest. But Damien shut with his own hand the door of his sepulchre."

The Government sent the lepers clothes and food

and then left them to themselves within their settlement to eke out a livelihood as best they could. The maxim was: "In this place there is no law, human or divine." They felt themselves outside the law and consequently, they gave themselves up to the terrible doctrines of the place. They grew reckless with despair. They threw all decency to the winds. They no longer cared. That they were "the devil's own brigade" seemed to be the burden of their song. They danced their dance of death on the brink of eternity and with pagan orgies of despair.

Man's heart is a deep of which he himself is often unaware. Lest they discover themselves they manufactured intoxicants from the roots of a plant which grew in the place, with results on their morals which may not be described on paper. Their clothes were far from being clean and decent on account of the scarcity of water. "Many a time," writes Damien, "in fulfilling my duties at their domiciles, I have been compelled to run outside to breathe the fresh air."

On the very first day of his arrival he took inventory of the surroundings. The dwellings of the unfortunate lepers were in a miserable condition; they were nothing but grass huts, unprotected in the rainy season, nothing but plague-stricken hovels. They had no separate abodes; they were all huddled together; the water supply was scanty, thus adding to the infection of the place. They were often in want of the necessaries of life. Little wonder that it was in the eyes of the natives a place with a shadow hanging over it.

It was, in truth, a place forgotten and cut off from the eyes of men. It seemed to be deserted by God till Damien came and raised the standard of the true Cross amidst the foul leper huts, and brought hope and joy and the touch of comradeship into their lives. His presence was as it were a sweet fragrance wafted from the meadow-lands of Heaven. They lifted up their souls in desire for better things when this big healthy brother of theirs dressed their wounds and poured the balm of a divine compassion on their bleeding souls. They knew him as their own. They began to pray, and to accept with patience their pitiable doom.

"In Molokai no tears are shed for they die within the brain.
Nothing abides but keenest pain, pain acute yet dead,
Pain as in a dream when the years go by, finally past and fugitive,
Where man lives, yet does not live or die."

He soon found his way into hearts which long years of suffering and despondency had sealed against all affection. Poor lepers who had no hope of a cure, their bodies doomed, were taught to raise their eyes on high—to believe that the patient bearing of their sad lot would win a reward exceeding great. Murmuring ceased, hope revived, and even the poor disfigured faces reflected the joy and peace that filled their minds. Damien was given the grace and the strength to stand before these outcasts and say, "You suffer, my children, take heart. Here in your midst is One who can turn your sorrow into joy. Go to Him, then, Who dwells in the Tabernacle. Go to Him. He will console you."

DAILY CONFLICT

*D*AMIEN at once set about his work of reform. He harassed the Government for better accommodations. He worked in company with the lepers building houses and soon six hundred cottages stood as the result of his endeavors. He next tackled the water supply. Hitherto water had to be carried from a gulch that was a very great distance from the center of the colony, and the more helpless lepers were able to procure a little only by begging from their healthier companions. He persisted in his demands for an adequate water supply and finally succeeded in getting a quantity of pipe which he lifted into position.

His tenacity of purpose was rewarded when a steady stream of clear, cold water began to pour into the village. He then improved the hospital, secured decent supplies of food and clothing, had a resident doctor appointed to visit the settlement occasionally . . . there was not a medicine chest in the entire colony before his time. His work soon became known outside and visitors called at the island.

But what a spectacle it was that met their gaze! Let us quote from the description given by Stevenson when he visited the island after the death of Damien: "When I was pulled ashore there one morning, there were with me in the boat two Sisters bidding farewell, in humble imitation of Damien, to the lights and joys of human life. One of them wept silently. I could not withhold myself from joining her. Had you been there it is my belief that nature would have triumphed even in you as the boat drew a little nearer, and you beheld the stairs crowded with abominable deformations of our common manhood and saw yourself landing in the midst of such a population as only now and then surrounds you in the horrors of a nightmare.

"Had you gone on . . . had you found every fourth face a blot on the landscape, had you visited the hospitals and found only butt ends of human beings lying there unrecognizable, but still breathing, still thinking, still remembering, you would have understood that life in the Lazarette is an ordeal from which the nerves of a man's spirit shrink even as his eye quails before the brightness of the sun. You would have felt that even to-day it is a pitiful place to visit, and a hell to live in. It is not the fear of possible infection; that seems a little thing in comparison with the pain, the pity, the disgust of the surroundings and the atmosphere of affliction, disease and physical disgrace in which one breathes."

Picture to yourself, then, a collection of huts filled with these lepers. There is no doctor there. In fact, as there is no cure there seems no place for a doctor's skill. Only the priest is their humble servant and does all the doctoring required.

Children were there—what a place for childhood which is usually connected with brightness and joy! —they presented the appearance of dwarfed old men. Stoddard, the first, by the way, who publicized the story of Damien's heroism, writes: . . . "a corner of the blanket was raised, the breathing object lay beneath, a human face turns slowly towards us, a face on which scarcely a trace of humanity remains. The dark skin was puffed up and blackened, a substance similar to a sort of glistening moss covered it, the muscles of the mouth had contracted and laid bare the grinning teeth, the thickened tongue lay like a fig between them, the eyelid, curled back, exposed the nerve surface, and protruding eye-balls, now shapeless and broken, look not unlike burst grapes. But enough of this. We can only assert there are sights there which one dare not describe—but which Damien saw, and breathed, and lived through with never a complaint, never a hint even, save vaguely, and what anyone could easily discover, as to the sights he met with in that place.

"If we could look out from these huts with the eyes of the sufferers, in their deep sorrow and despair as they watched this strong man moving about among their hovels; if we heard the whispers of wonder and astonishment that one could be found to come and live his life among them, you would know something of the love that went out from their hearts for this great big brother of theirs—aye, and our brother, too."

"AS ONE WHO SERVES"

$\mathcal{L}$ET US follow Damien as he goes about his daily work. His letters reveal the story: "It is indeed in tears that I sow the good seed from morning till night among my poor lepers. I am in the midst of physical and moral miseries which rend my heart. Nevertheless, I endeavor to show myself always cheerful that I may raise the courage of the weak. I place death before their eyes as the end of all their evils, if they are willing to be sincere converts. Many in consequence look upon death with resignation and sometimes with joy.

"Every morning, after offering the Holy Sacrifice of the Mass, I go to visit the sick, half of whom are Catholics. Everyone, with the exception of a few bigoted heretics, looks upon me as a father. As for me, I make myself a leper with the lepers to gain all to Christ. This is why in preaching I say 'we lepers' instead of 'my brethren.' People pity me and think me unfortunate, but I think of myself as the happiest of missionaries."

The average death-rate was now about one every day. Many were so destitute that there was no means available to defray the expenses of burial. The dead were simply wrapped in a blanket. Four lepers, who would probably in the not too distant future expect a like courtesy towards themselves, volunteer to carry the corpse to its last resting place. Damien was shocked when he learned that the grave was nothing but a shallow ditch dug just deep enough to receive the body. Into this it was unceremoniously deposited with the least amount of trouble. He was still further shocked to learn that at night wild dogs, and even swine, prowled around the graveyard. His Catholic soul revolted at the desecrations. With shovel and ax he set to work on the burial ground until the appalling conditions were somewhat, for the moment, rectified.

He with his own hands dug graves that were at least six feet deep, and constructed a supply of coffins for which there was a daily demand. He was a carpenter, a mason, a doctor, a nurse, a father, a mother, ready for any work that his hand might do. Damien was none of your snowy-white, delicate-handed dilettante priests. "To counteract the bad smell, I made myself accustomed to the use of tobacco . . . on many occasions the smell of my pipe was my preservation, and saved me from carrying on my clothes the noxious smell of the lepers." We are glad he had that pipe! We gather more broken details from his letters home, for he loved the homeland and the pleasant places in Tremoloo. "All repugnance for the lepers has ceased. The weekly visit to my parishioners takes four or five days."

Two meals a day were his limit. A late morning meal, consisting of rice, meat, coffee and a few 'hardtack' biscuits and in the evening "what was left from dinner, with a cup of tea, the water for which I boil over a lamp. You see, I live very well; I do not starve and I am not much at home in the daytime." Towards evening he would light the lamp, read his breviary, write to his dear ones at Tremoloo or read again the precious letters sent from there, or he might stroll in the graveyard adjoining his dwelling-place. "The cemetery, church and my house form but one enclosure," he wrote to Pamphile, "thus at night I am the sole keeper of this garden of the dead where my poor children lie at rest."

Often he would stroll thus among the graves, saying his beads and "meditating on the unending happiness which so many of them are now enjoying. I confess to you, my brother, the cemetery and the huts of the dying are my best meditation books."

Stoddard, the American author who visited him, gives us details of the Sunday Mass. "The neatly robed sanctuary boys were all disfigured, some with pitifully distorted features, fingers and toes missing, in many cases eyelids thickened and out of shape. The very richly wrought golden vessels used in the service were sent to him from Paris. With great sweetness and simplicity the celebrant proceeded with the celebration of the Holy Sacrifice in the presence of this strange other-world congregation.

"All of them seemed to be singing, or trying to sing, simple refrains that sounded strangely enough from the hoarse throats of the singers. The devotion of the place was remarkable. What a contrast was here to be witnessed . . . the bright altar cleanly furnished, the young priest the picture of health, at his side the acolytes on whose infant features was already fixed the certain seal of early death, beyond the altar rails corruption ran riot, there was scarcely a form in that whole congregation from which one would not turn away in horror, and many of the worshippers seemed to have risen from the corruption of the grave. The rhythmic boom of the sea-surf was fitting accompaniment to that solemn scene, and the long, low sigh of the sea-wind was like a note of sympathy.

"Yet, do not our hearts go out to this heroic priest with feeling deeper than pity, stronger than love? We would not have spared him one single horror, we would not give him any rest or relaxation, or any sweetening of the Chalice, or any drugging of the gall . . . and yet again, we would. But alas, we can only stand afar off and watch Damien the Priest . . . and his Sacrifice . . . And as we watch we seem to catch upon his features the lineaments of another One Who became a leper . . . wounds, and bleeding, and swelling sores . . . We stop, beggared for words."
Thus writes Stoddard!

TRIUMPH OF FAITH

RELIGION seems to have been put to the test here. When one remembers what Molokai was before Damien came, and how he purged it of its dark and bloody rites, and its wild nights of sin, one can form some idea of the long and relentless struggle he endured in crushing out the evil influences which led these unfortunate lepers to be, even when face to face with death, victims of the most revolting superstitions. He possessed as heritage from his Flemish ancestry a more than ordinary courage and a determination that was only intensified by opposition.

This combined with his intrepid faith and zeal for the cause of God made him irresistible in his efforts to inspire the people with trust in God and in the consolations of the Christian religion. Slowly but surely he led them to a better mood and a higher hope. Before he came, the dying were cast out of the huts and laid behind a stone wall and left there to die in the ditch like some poor animal that could not feel, nor suffer, nor think within its brain.

Then after death's merciful release they were flung into the grave without a prayer or any token of a new life. Now there was reverence for the dead, which meant a stirring of hope; and, strengthened by their faith, men waited for death as a prisoner waits for the unlocking of the prison-door. It brought release and triumph. No longer was the body treated as a vile thing; now they learned to see in it the dwelling-place of the Spirit of God.

The funeral cortege was like a glad procession accompanied with music. Not in vain did Damien plant the Cross on this lonely outpost watch, for it alone gave an answer and a cure. The poor people seemed to catch his own spirit of generosity and responded in the way that pleased him best. The churches were filled and each Sunday morning saw a lengthening stream of lepers approach the altar rail. "My lepers," he writes, "are very fervent. They fill the church from morn till night and pour forth their prayers to God with an ardor that would make some religious blush. Some of them have learned to offer themselves as victims for the sins of the world."

The Corpus Christi processions were a big event. Along the wayside were lined the more stricken people while the healthier ones carried the canopy or walked reverently before it. These adoring lepers bring us back to those other days in Palestine when 'Jesus of Nazareth was passing by.' There were sights there to move a strong man's feelings . . . bands of little children flinging fragrant flowers towards the gleaming monstrance and singing in their native tongue a hymn with words like these perhaps:

"How long shall I be captive in this strange land
Where night and day weeping is my portion,
And all my bread is bitter tears?
When shall I see my well-beloved Lord . . .
Guardian of my soul, my Saviour, my hope,
    my All?"

Was it not worth while, after all, that he had come? His heart went out to the children. As he wrote: "It is painful to see oneself surrounded by these unfortunate children, but I derive much consolation from them."

The Molokai to which Damien came was a foul place wherein the code was "here there is no law, human or divine;" it was not long before the grace of God was working wonders . . . a Guild of Perpetual Adoration was established in that most abandoned spot on earth, and at every hour of the long day, lepers knelt and adored the hidden Saviour Who had not disdained to become for love of them "a leper and no man." Confraternities of the Sick and of the Dying were erected and now no longer was any one of them desolate in the hour of his extremity.

TOUCHSTONE OF SUCCESS

*T*HOUGH Damien had won the love and reverence of his friends the lepers, he had, strange to say, his enemies. And yet why do we say strange? It was the bitter chalice of his Master. "The servant is not above His Lord." Some of these enemies were ministers of other religions who were jealous of him. Jealous of him!

Often he had to fight his way with narrow-minded officials who did not love the faith he so loyally professed. And sometimes he came into collision with the police and others in league with those who concocted the intoxicating liquor from the *Ki* root. He knew what it was to be persecuted for justice's sake. We know now that his work was silently as well as openly thwarted. Not until it became known to the outside world that he had contracted the dread disease did his adversaries become ashamed and cease from troubling him.

He certainly was not popular with the officials in Molokai. "He was a difficult man to work with," says one. "A good man, but very officious," said another.

"Obstinate, brusque, and overbearing," said a third. We are trying to see Damien as he was. And we thank God Who blessed him with a strong head as well as with a warm heart. He had his faults. He probably was a poor manager, was ever determined to get his own way for the sake of his unfortunate lepers, and he sometimes lost his temper. But despite these human limitations he stands alone, crowned with glory and honors, lauded wherever good men band together for the succor of the defenceless, and this because he toiled and suffered and endured in that miserable hut of his under the cliffs of Kalanao.

Our indignation is rightly aroused as we read of the reception his appeals for help met with from the officials of the Board of Health in Honolulu. They hailed Damien as an officious busy-body, declared his petitions for means of alleviating the lepers' miseries "of no concern of his,—his ministrations should begin and end with the spiritual care of the Catholics in Molokai." Yes, Damien lost his temper. He minced no words in telling these officials where their functions began and where they should end.

And we are sorry to read of the *manifesto* later issued by this same Board of Health to the effect that only lepers destined for the colony were to be landed from the steamers, that nobody from the settlement was to be permitted to have contact in any way with ships anchored off the shore, that cargo for the settlement was to be dumped into open boats or on an isolated section of the shore, . . . and Damien was warned: "if you ever appear here again, or even so much as cross the mountains that separate the leper colony from the rest of the island you will be arrested and jailed like any other felon." But, he usually succeeded in getting what he wanted, even from the Board of Health.

However, it was from the charity of the Bishop and the well-disposed residents of Honolulu who raised funds by popular subscription that he was finally enabled to secure building materials and tools for the erection of the cottages needed by the poor lepers. Until his death, Damien had to contend with unsympathetic officials, and not a single improvement in the colony was accomplished without exceeding difficulty.

As a result of this bickering with the authorities, he was forbidden by the Home Secretary to set foot outside the settlement and was declared a State prisoner. It had been his custom to go occasionally to Honolulu to make his confession and to confer with the Bishop. He protested often but in vain this cruel enactment against his liberty. He even pleaded with these unsympathetic and vindictive officials, protesting his necessity of seeing a fellow-priest occasionally. This was the time of his sorest trial.

The Bishop on one occasion took a steamer bound for Molokai, anxious to visit his exiled priest. The captain refused to allow him to land. Father Damien saw the ship at anchor and at once put out in a canoe with two lepers. He was not allowed on board. Then was witnessed a scene worthy of a great painter's touch—Father Damien standing in his little boat before high heavens, under the beetling crags, with seagulls circling about, making aloud the confession of all his faults and failings and receiving absolution from the bishop in yonder steamer. The recording angel must have brushed aside a tear as he handed in the account. The steamer moved on. Damien returned to his lepers.

Soon after this incident the unjust prohibition was partly withdrawn and Damien was allowed to visit other parts of the island.

About a year later a resident priest came to occupy a church built by Damien on the other end of the island, and to minister to the non-leper residents. Damien's visits to Honolulu became thus unnecessary, and so he practically renounced the natural claims of existence, "to seek and to save that which was lost."

SOURCE OF HIS CONSOLATION

*W*HAT strikes one in reading the meagre accounts recorded of Damien is his simplicity of character. He was not fond of speaking of himself, just giving the scantiest details of his life. A great man clothed with humility. His letters home were very human documents. His mother wrote him as all mothers will, God bless them! advising him to be careful and to mind himself. But her boy had long since gone beyond our comfortable ways of thought. He sent her a cheerful letter, making inquiries about little details at home, telling her not to worry, he was all right. "I live all alone in my little hut, the lepers never enter it." His pipe became more and more his companion. . . .

Wasn't it just as well that he spared the old lady at Tremoloo, that he kept from her the horrors of the life he really led? His letters were great by their silence. The infinite is often best expressed by trivialities, by the unsaid word. He had no news to relate. No news, indeed! He had ever great love for the homeland and his kindred, but Tremoloo was no longer home for him. Not a day passes, so he writes his mother, without paying her a visit in spirit.

He fills his letters with questions concerning the old, familiar, homely things . . . it would be real winter weather there now . . . the River Laak would be frozen to a hardness that would delight the lover of skating . . . he wonders if Mother still uses the trusty stick to help her pick her way to Mass. . . . In his solitary hours sitting under the friendly pandanus tree on the lonely island prison, while listening to the surf boom on the cliffs, his thoughts defied time and space and were wafted back to homeland, the old familiar faces, and often, at eventide, as he walked home under the stars he thought of the stars which shone above his father's house, recalling in all the rosiest colors of his dreams the little Flemish village, the shades of evening falling on the plain, the soothing rustle of sound in the snug farmyard, the farmhouse kitchen where the welcome fire would be blazing, the polished copper and delf glistening on the whitewashed walls, the tender l o v i n g faces wreathed in smiles and, crowning all, the dear, gray head of his revered mother.

However, Damien indulged no flights of fancy, no emotional extravagances. But he did pray. It was in the silent atmosphere of his little chapel he found the super-human strength to face the duties of each new dawn. It was there before the Blessed Sacrament he found the courage to smile at shrinking fears, to look into the future with courage, to help other men see this vision too. He was no stranger to that devastating loneliness which is of the spirit. "Without the Blessed Sacrament," he writes, "a life like mine would be intolerable, but with the Blessed Sacrament I am always gay and work cheerfully for the relief of the poor lepers." We know what that little sentence means. All his secret life was crushed into these few words . . . his weakness, his strength, his high resolve, his sense of need, of friendship, of human understanding.

It gives us an insight into his heart as he worked and chatted, always with the vision of Christ before him, and the hunger in his heart to do Christ's work among the outcast. That was his comfort as he wended his lonely way to the huts of the plague-stricken, or walked at eventide beside the restless sea. Everywhere in his journeyings up and down the colony he felt this presence of his Lord.

And so it came to pass that for Damien the Gospel-story was not far-off history but an ever-present event. His daily life became very vividly a walking in the company of the Master. By faith he saw these lepers gathered about the person of Christ. In his daily walks he met only . . . lepers!

After long years on the island, after much seeking and craving, he secured the assistance of other priests, as well as three nuns, and two lay-brothers. There was an Irish Brother there, tall, auburn-haired, generous-hearted, named Brother James. The moment he had learned in far-away Australia that there were deeds of daring still to be achieved, that they were actually being achieved by a humble Belgian missionary, he boarded the first outbound vessel from Sydney and landed in Molokai where he pledged himself to assist Damien.

We are glad that an Irishman was there. With the ardor and generosity of the Celt, Brother James devoted himself utterly to the personal service of Damien who was now so much in need. Brother James' life was bound up henceforth in Damien; he never seemed to be able to do enough for him. Thus in the evening of his days did God bless Damien with the one thing most completely absent from his life in the colony, human friendship. His work, too, was insured against destruction.

A middle-aged ex-soldier from the United States named Dutton, Joseph Dutton, read of the self-sacrificing life Damien was leading in the island prison of Molokai. Dutton was in search of a more perfect way to the Kingdom of God. "Sell all, give it to the poor . . . and . . . follow Me." This was the direct instruction of the Master; it was exemplified in the life of Damien. Dutton, too, at one time dreamed of a solitary way, of hard toil, of physical renunciations, such as might be found among austere Trappist monks, but after a short probation there the story of Damien's heroic venture fell into his hands. His quest for the higher life could end. He had found his true vocation. He stayed with Damien to the end, and long years after found him untiring in his devotion to the unfortunate lepers of Molokai.

In the Catholic Encyclopedia, an account of Molokai is given by this marvelous Dutton. He says in part: "It is the name of Damien that has made Molokai known throughout the whole world. He came to the Settlement to remain in May, 1873. Good order in the settlement was somewhat precarious, but Damien's determined character proved to be of great value. Besides his priestly office, there was opportunity for his efforts at every turn. With a hungry zeal for work he accomplished many things for the good of the place; he helped the authorities and brought about a good spirit among the people.

"Ten years later, in 1883, Damien strained every effort to secure the help of Sisters . . . at that time the conditions would indeed have been intolerable, as they still were when the writer (Dutton) joined Damien. Finally, in 1888, Franciscan Sisters came from Syracuse, New York. In 1889, Damien died and his death, after such a life, arrested the world's attention. A spontaneous outburst of applause from everywhere at once followed. The sixteen years that Damien spent in Molokai made a record that seemed unique to the world at large.

"Father Damien's life came as a startling revelation of heroic self-sacrifice. He is acknowledged the Apostle of the lepers and whatever any others may do in the same field will help to perpetuate his fame and hon-

or." This tribute from one who worked side by side with Damien needs no comment.

To these devoted friends were added the long-desired community of Sisters. It seemed as if all Damien's hopes were being realized. The Sisters initiated a regime of cleanliness as well as the establishment of a modern clinic for the dressing of the lepers' sores. A Girls' Home was placed under their supervision and, in general, things were never so bright. . . . But, one evening when, as was his wont, Brother James was getting ready a bath of hot water to bathe Father Damien's feet when he returned footsore and weary after the day's toil, in a moment of abstraction Damien put his foot into the boiling water . . . and felt no pain.

"Are you scalded?" asked Brother James, anxiously.

Both men looked at each other. Came in that tense moment the realization: Damien was a leper!

"Ah! must—

Designer infinite!

Ah must Thou char the wood ere Thou canst limn with it?"

Pain, suffering, darkness, these are messengers of God to the soul attuned to divine realities. God loves not to afflict, yet He spared not His only Son. The mystery of suffering will always defy explanation in human language, but sometimes as in the case of St. Francis of Assisi the message can be read even in the mortal flesh. It is ever the final seal of God's predilection since the spotless and lifegiving Victim hung crucified on the Tree. "And I, if I be lifted up, will draw all things to Myself." Damien's life-work would be incomplete if he had escaped that final seal of suffering. Molokai was definitely redeemed by the humble priest who refused not to become a counterpart of the Crucified.

THE FINAL STAND

$\mathcal{D}$AMIEN a leper! One at last in suffering as he had ever been one in sympathy. He was in very deed a prisoner now with the others. And in that hour he was not afraid. It was the bargain he had made long ago when he had passed that first night under the spreading pandanus tree; it was the doom he sought. He inquired from the doctor.

The verdict was conclusive. The kindly Doctor hesitated: "I cannot bear to tell you what you know is the case."

But Damien with decision answered: "It is no shock, for a long time now I have felt sure of this."

For eleven years Damien had gone among his people as a serving man, "in the midst of them as one that serveth," attending their sick, making their coffins, burying their dead, yet never by an act or word showing that he considered his services as being in any way heroic. One of his first improvements in the island had been the renovating of the 'hospital,' a shed which served really as a species of morgue. Here in varying states of decomposition the friendless dying were dumped to spend their last hours of life out of sight of passersby.

Damien had the building remodelled, installed cots, secured the services of a few of the more healthy lepers to act as nurses, while he fulfilled the office of doctor, personally attending to the sores and bandages of each inmate. This self-imposed task was of daily occurrence until two years before his own death. Damien was now a leper. The wonder was that he had escaped so long.

"I am glad. There is no doubt about my sickness. I am a leper," was his word to his brother Pamphile. He had found the secret of all joy—though face to face with the vision of his Gethsemane—the secret of Christ, which is self-denial.

As a ship-wrecked man on the rocks watches the sea rising inch by inch, he saw the tide of leprosy rising within his veins, watched its daily, slow, deliberate advance. He had long since flung down defiance in the face of death—he had no fears, and the disease found him unafraid 'as a tool in the hands of a skillful workman.' But though Damien joined the ranks of the afflicted, he never relaxed his energies, nor permitted himself any concessions, nor did he devote any extra care to himself during the five years that remained to him.

Writing to his bishop he said, "I cannot go to Honolulu, there are signs of the disease on my left cheek and ear, and my eyebrows are beginning to fall. I shall soon be quite disfigured. I have no real doubt as to the character of my malady, so I remain

60

calm, resigned, and very happy in the midst of my people. The good God knows what is best for my sanctification, and I say daily, 'Thy Will be done,' with a ready heart. The Government has entrusted me with the building of a large hospital so now I have to work not alone as priest and doctor, but also as architect."

When it was flashed across the world that Damien was a leper, it stirred the hearts of the people beyond the island, and men waited, and watched, and held their breath as if a friend were holding rendezvous with death in the next room. The picture of Father Damien as stricken with leprosy was exposed in the window of a photographer's shop in Bond Street, London. Its repulsiveness was so great that at first people shrank from the very sight of it. No sooner, however, was it known that this was Father Damien's picture than the spectators blocked the traffic to look upon the face of this man who was brother of all suffering humanity.

Newman's *credo* holds for every man, in every age: "I believe and by Thy grace will ever believe and hold, and I know that it is true, that nothing great is done without suffering, without humiliation, and that all things are possible by means of it. . . . O my dear Lord, though I am so very weak that I am not fit to ask Thee for suffering as a gift, and have not strength to do so, at least I will beg of Thee grace to meet suffering well when Thou in Thy love and wisdom dost bring it upon me."

WHITE MARTYRDOM

"THERE is Red martyrdom and White martyrdom," wrote an Irish monk one day on his parchment scroll. "Red martyrdom is achieved when one gives up his life for a sacred cause, white martyrdom is the daily dying to oneself." The slow death of Damien smote him piece by piece. This dying by inches called back again to our modern times the high spirit of the arena days.

Following is a description of his personal appearance shortly before his death: a thick-set and strongly-built man, with black curly hair and short beard turning gray. His countenance must have been handsome, with a firm, well-curved mouth, but he is now disfigured a good deal by leprosy, yet not so badly as to make it anything but a pleasure to look on his bright animated face. His forehead is swollen and ridged, the eyebrows gone, the ears greatly enlarged. "There is no beauty nor comeliness that we should desire in him."

But though the disease made rapid progress, he was energetic as ever, though no longer able to go on his long fatiguing journeys. He writes: "I am still able to stand at the Altar though with considerable difficulty. I do not forget any one of you. Do you in return pray for me and secure prayers from others for me who am being so gently drawn, day by day, to the tomb. And may the good God strengthen us."

Concerning his Mass as a leper—he regards it as a blessing of Providence that the fingers which held the chalice were not afflicted with the disease. Oh, for power to portray the exquisite beauty of that poor bandaged leper hand, a worthy hand!

> *"Oh, God, the purest offering*
> *Of tainted earth below,*
> *Unblushing to Thy feet we bring—*
> *A leper white as snow."*

His last letter from Molokai: "I try my best to go on without much complaining and to accept in a practical way for my soul's sake the long-foreseen miseries of the disease. I try to make slowly my Way of the Cross and hope soon to be on top of my Golgotha."

Of course the other inhabitants of the island knew that Damien was long a-dying in their midst but, when the news was actually flashed abroad that he was on his death-bed, a cry of wailing arose in the land. The door of his little hut was ever open; the sweet fragrance of the honey-suckle was wafted towards the poor dying man; messengers came at every hour enquiring for him, showing in their sincere and halting fashion their loyal and enduring sympathy. He would have no tears, however, and usually had a joke or a cheery word for every one.

His visitors marvelled at his unalterable patience. He who had been so strong, so active, so ardent, was now nailed to his miserable couch. The Sisters were in constant attendance at that lowly deathbed while Brother James was his loyal faithful nurse. How poorly off he was! He who had spent so much money to relieve the lepers had so forgotten himself that he had none of the comforts, scarcely even the necessities of life. Sometimes he suffered intensely, sometimes was mercifully unconscious.

As he lay there in his wooden shed with the roar of the sea sounding ever more faintly in his dying ear, and the kindly face of the good Brother working with sorrow beside him, what were his thoughts? . . .

"They are all gone," said he, referring to the lepers who had met and welcomed him on that never-to-be-forgotten first day in the colony, "and I shall be seeing them soon." He asked that the natives be allowed to sing his favorite hymn:

"When, oh, when shall it be given me to behold
my God,
How long shall I be captive in this strange land?"

On April 13, 1889, he died, without a struggle, as if falling asleep; bearing upon his body honorable

64

wounds, while the soul of Joseph Damien de Veuster rose like a lark to its God. His beautiful, pure soul was in the presence of Him he had loved and served so well. The bell was tolled. A long, low wail rose along the cliffs. The father and friend of the lepers was dead. Death, yes. But not defeat. It was glorious, magnificent, triumphant victory. The young lad of Tremoloo had walked into history, into a place among the great ones, and is now evermore the exemplar of noble deeds. He was laid to rest under the shade of the friendly pandanus tree which had sheltered him the first night he slept within sound of the seas. "I would like to rest by the side of my church, under the stout old tree where I rested so many nights before I had any other shelter." His request was reverently complied with.

Though he no longer rests in the solitary settlement of Molokai, the accompanying sonnet by Mary Quinlan, an Irish writer, will not be out of place.

"No golden dome shines over Damien's sleep.
A leper's grave upon a leprous strand
Where hope is dead and hand must shrink from
    hand,
Where cataracts wail towards a mournful deep
And frowning purple cliffs in mercy keep
All wholesome life at distance, hath God planned
For him who led the saints' heroic band
And died a shepherd of Christ's exiled sheep.

"O'er Damien's dust the broad skies bend for dome
Stars burn for golden letters and the sea
Shall roll perpetual anthem round his rest,
For Damien made the charnal-house life's home
Matched love with death—and Damien's name shall
  be
A glorious possession, world-possest."

On February 3, 1936, at the request of the Belgian government, the body of Damien was translated to the Chapel of the Fathers of the Sacred Heart, Louvain, Belgium. Amid the wailing and tears of the faithful lepers of Molokai the body was taken from its grave under the shade of the pandanus tree, and with unheard-of acclaim, full liturgical pomp and royal salutes, was escorted to the waiting American steamer while the Stars and Stripes dipped in homage to the world-hero.

At San Francisco, the precious body of the erstwhile leper was again given a welcome unparalleled in magnificence. Finally, at Panama the American Navy resigned its honored trust to the Commander of the Belgian flagship, and Damien returned home at last. At Antwerp, the King of the Belgians met the solemn cortege in company with the Cardinal Archbishop of Malines. In Belgium he will receive honors which the poor lepers of Molokai may not bestow . . . but his glory will ever be that he achieved white martyrdom in Molokai.

Fearless, serene, undaunted, he stands out an example. True, we cannot all be Damiens. But perhaps it will be profitable to measure ourselves with the man, to feel how puny we are in our ordered, selfish ways, and resolve that in our own sphere, wherever we are, his burning example will help us play the man and act well our part. In times of stress let us remember Damien as he was on that first night on the island of Molokai when he made his first great sacrifice.

Let us remind ourselves again and yet again that the high romance and sweeping adventure of life lies not alone on strange mountains nor on uncharted seas, nor on the palm-girdled isles of the Pacific—it is often on the road before our doors; it is to be found in the faces and hearts of unheralded pilgrims who meet up with us on our plodding way. Let us remember that the same moon that lights up the roadways of our cherished homeland tonight will shine over the whitewashed leper huts in numerous leper colonies to light up the pathway of the consecrated Sisters and Brothers and Priests passing like ministering angels up and down that land of pain. These tread in the footprints of Damien and help smooth the pillows of this dying race of men.

Then, perhaps, we may learn the lesson torn from the very heart of life, the lesson of all wisdom, the lesson that comes to us trembling from the strings and 'across the sweetest passage of a song,' that our life here is only great or good or beautiful or tender by virtue of its sacrifice, by virtue of each one denying himself for the sake of Christ's little ones, His least brethren.

DAMIEN'S MESSAGE

$\mathcal{D}$AMIEN opened the window of the world on the misery of Molokai. To all of us his life is a challenge and an appeal to do our part for our helpless brethren in the leper colonies of the far-flung Pacific. To do it unselfishly, and in his large way. Damien solved the social problem as Christ solved it—by giving himself. There is no cure for the world's ills unless it comes with Christ's blessing upon it, unless it comes tempered with His mercy, His justice, and His love. "There is no need," writes Rene Bazin, "to go searching for a remedy for the evils of the times . . . the remedy already exists. It is the giving of oneself to those who have fallen so low that even hope fails them. Open wide your heart, love the sinner whatever his sin be, forgive, however ignorant he may be—he does not understand."

Damien's life is like moral dynamite to blow away our selfishness—like a whip to sting us into unselfish work for those who cannot help themselves—like a beacon to guide us on the road of Christian charity. We must remember in all our dealing with the unfortunate that kindness is often, nay, always, a greater gift than gold. Indeed, all the wealth of the Indies, all the treasures of Araby could not price the heroism of that lonely martyr's life. It was a check only to be cashed across the counters of Heaven. Damien's sacrifice was grand and beautiful as a work of God, filling all the earth with beauty as when the sinking sun makes of the distant horizon one blaze of glory, flooding the land with its mellow golden light; or again like a sweet-toned bell flinging its liquid notes on the mellow evening air.

He was a man whose faith and love were bells of full accord, ringing clearly on the air a message to the world: "Greater love than this no man hath than that a man lay down his life for his friend." "What are men thinking of?" he once questioned, as did another hero of God—Xavier—in another age. What are men thinking of? A padded life of ease where the wheels go smoothly along without jog or jar— or does the story of Damien engender the resolve to make the world a better place for their having lived in it?

If, as the Apostle says, "it is good to think on what is high, and holy, and of good repute," surely it will do us good to warm our souls on the memory of this hero of our faith, for the echo of his life will roll from soul to soul like a bugle call on the hill.

We believe in the aristocracy of souls. Thanks to Damien and his dream we have our heroic priests and devoted Sisters in Molokai today. Nor is that island alone in its service to the out-cast. The flame of zeal has been set aburning in other hearts and in many lands . . . we have not alone Molokai but Culion and Cebu in the Philippines, and a host of other blessed havens where the keynote of service is the Master's "Amen, amen I say to you, what you have done for the least of these, My little ones, you have done it unto Me."

Tread softly, all who walk life's corridors. The world is a hospital and open are its doors, and within, souls await the sweet balm of comfort, a ray of light to cheer their darkened way, a word of peace to soothe their troubled hearts. May this sketch of the life of Damien the Leper touch us all to finer pity and help to keep our hearts attuned to the sufferings of the poor. This is our reason for writing on Damien. To point out the quiet bravery of simple holy lives, the beauty that comes to souls when duty is humbly done, the pathos, the love, the strength we can achieve through the faith, to prove that even here and now suffering is fraught with meaning for every man, for every nation.

Of Damien it may be truly said:
*"He died for a dream born in a herdsman's shed,
And for the secret scripture of the poor."*

ABOUT THE AUTHOR

FATHER John Henaghan, St. Columban missionary, was killed in Manila on February 10, 1945, leaving to those who follow him a legacy of rare spirituality, expressed in poetic prose. Father Henaghan was ordained in Maynooth in 1909, a classmate of Bishop Galvin, founder of St. Columban's. He left the archdiocese of Tuam in Ireland, to join his classmate in the new misson Society and became Editor of the Irish *Far East* in 1918. Immediately his ardent spiritual editorials, characterized by a vigorous, novel approach to ancient truths, attracted wide attention. This was old wine in new bottles. He seemed to have a predilection for Father Damien long before he saw the mission fields and gave glowing lectures on this martyr of charity. Shortly before his death, when his fame as a man of deep spirituality was known and evident to all, his humility forced him to write complainingly to a friend: "How dry, how wooden, how commonplace, how poor my soul really is. When I speak of Him, I can be authentic and confident; I know what He can do . . . but I am too heavy, too spiritually slothful, too dull . . . Doesn't it seem a contradiction—a kind of Jekyll and Hyde affair? But really that is the truth about me."